The Stones of Venice

THE

STONES OF VENICE.

𝔓lates.

By JOHN RUSKIN,

AUTHOR OF "THE SEVEN LAMPS OF ARCHITECTURE," "MODERN PAINTERS," ETC., ETC.

NEW YORK:
JOHN WILEY & SONS,
No. 15 ASTOR PLACE.
1880.

LIST OF PLATES.

Wall-Veil Decoration.

CA' TREVISAN CA' DARIO.

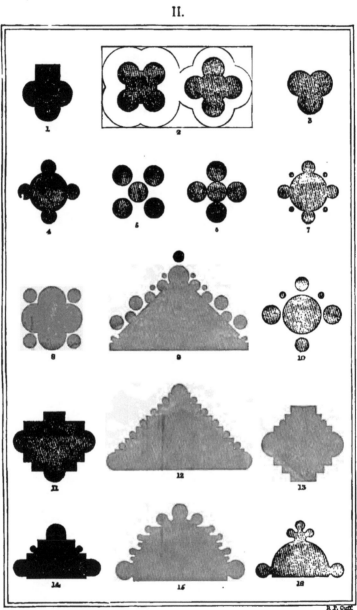

Plans of Piers.

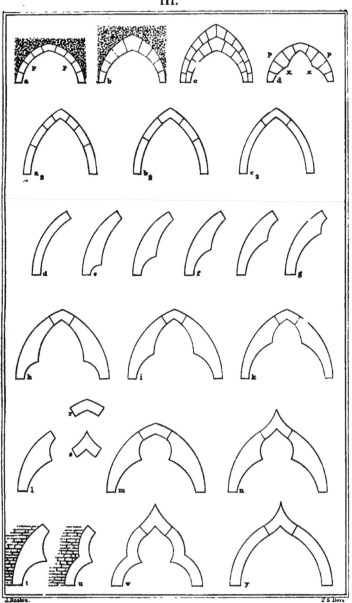

Arch Masonry.

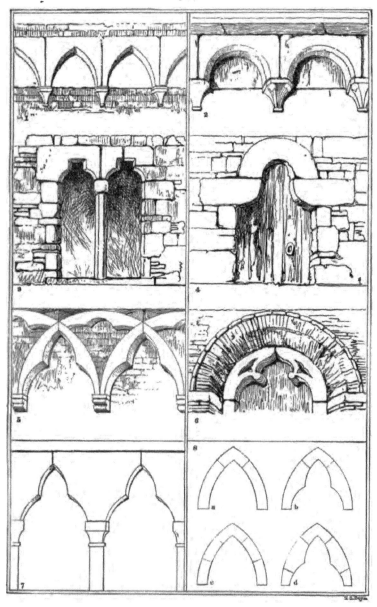

Arch Masonry.

Arch Masonry.

BROLETTO OF COMO

HARROUN & BIERSTADT. N. Y.

Types of Towers.

VII.

Decoration by Disks.

PALAZZO DEI BADOARI PARTECIPAZZIA.

Edge Decoration.

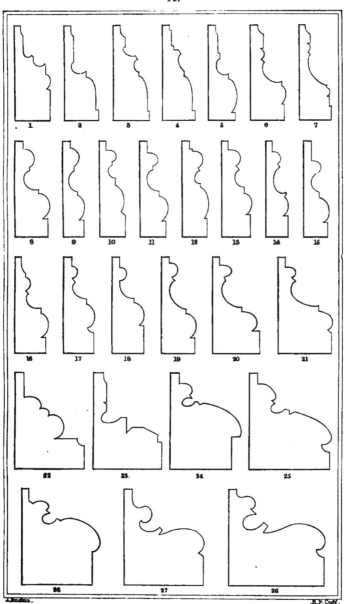

Profiles of Bases.

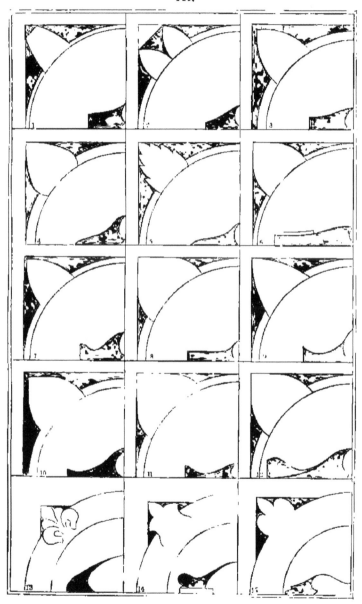

Plans of Bases.

HARROUN & SIERSTADT. N. Y.

Decoration of Bases.

Spandril Decoration.

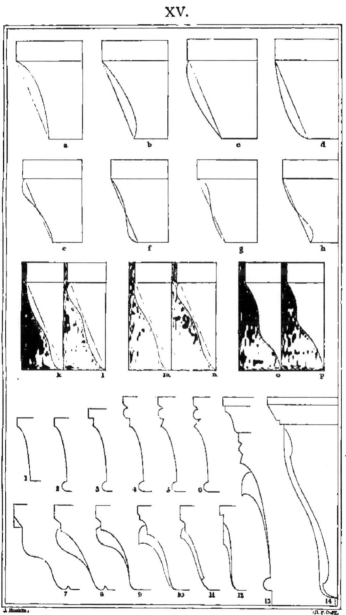

Cornice Profiles.

ARTOTYPE

HARROUN & BIERSTADT, N. Y.

Cornice Decoration.

ARTOTYPE

HARROUN & BIERSTADT, N. Y.

Capitals.

CONVEX GROUP.

Artshaft Decoration.

Wall-Veil Decoration.

CA' TREVISAN.

XX.

LIST OF PLATES.

- - -- — ---

I.

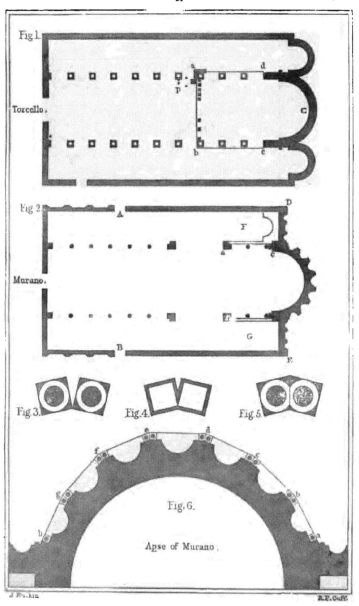

Plans of Torcello and Murano.

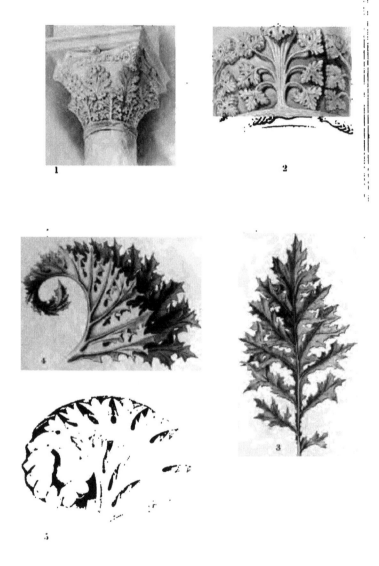

The Acanthus of Torcello.

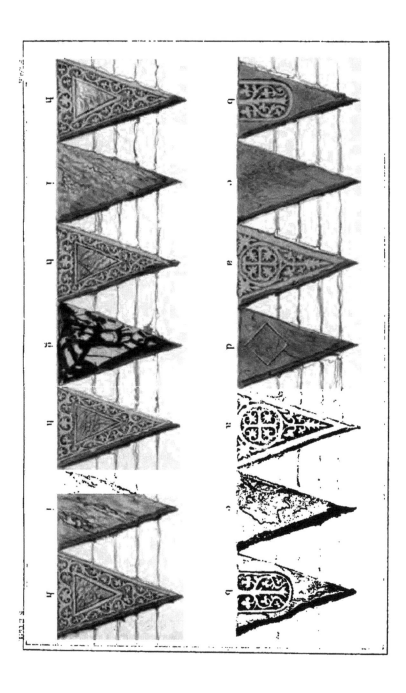

Sculptures of Murano.

Archivolt in the Duomo of Murano

ARTOTYPE

MAGHOLN & H·H·FAUT. N·Y

The Vine. Free, and in Service.

Byzantine Capitals. Convex Group.

HARROUN & BIERSTADT. N. Y.

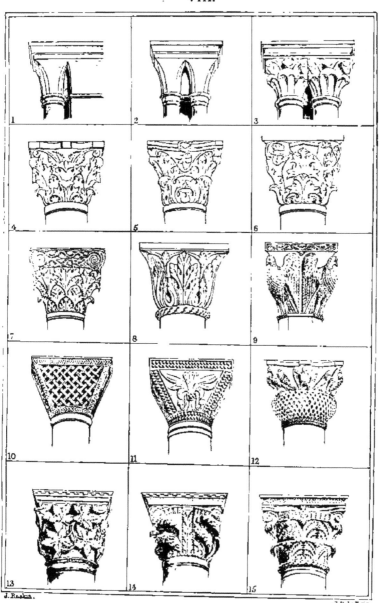

Byzantine Capitals. Concave Group.

Lily Capital of St. Mark's.

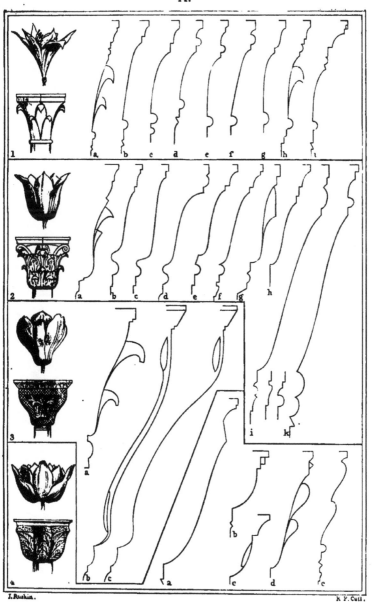

J. Ruskin.

K. F. Cuff.

The Four Venetian Flower Orders.

2 1 3

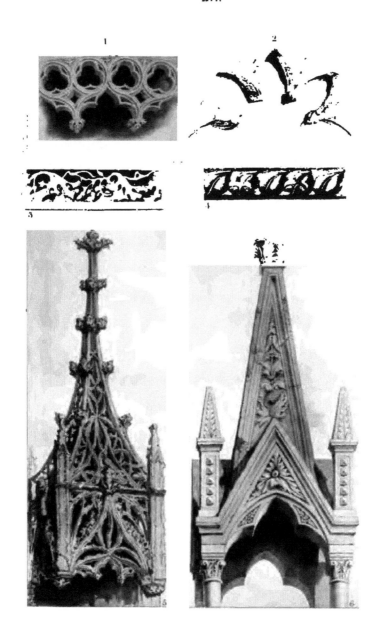

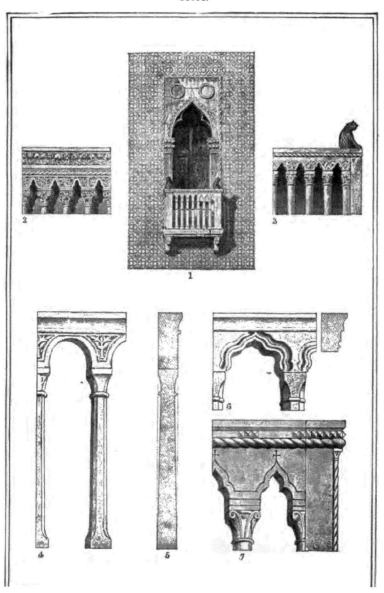

XIV.

J. Ruskin.

R. P. Cuff.

The Orders of Venetian Arches.

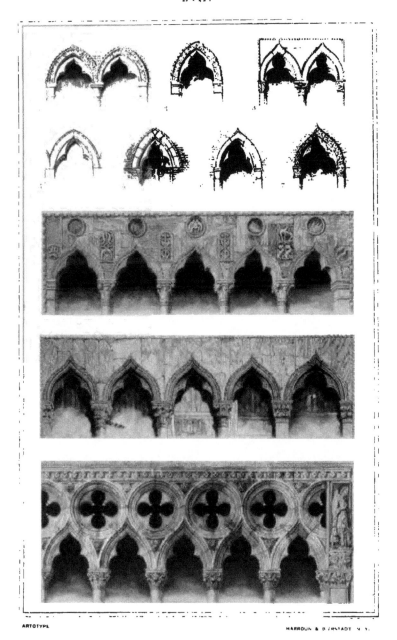

Windows of the Early Gothic Palaces.

Windows of the Fifth Order.

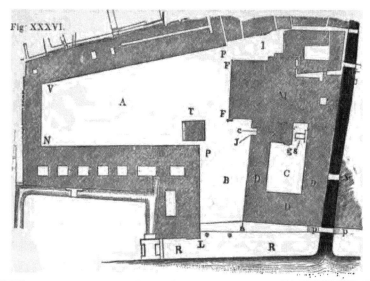

Fig. XXXVI.

Fig. XXXVII.

Leafage of the Vine Angle.

Leafage of the Venetian Capitals.

LIST OF PLATES.

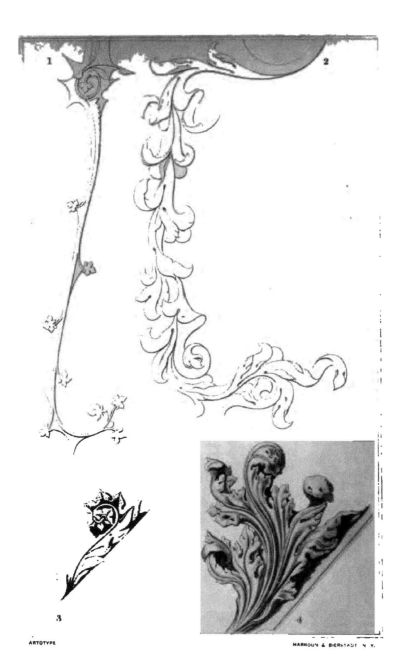

HARROUN & BIERSTADT N. Y.

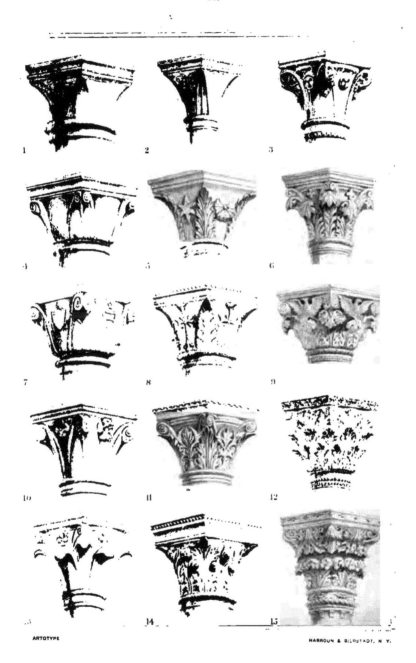

HARROUN & BILRSTADT, N. Y.

Gothic Capitals.

III

Mosaics of Olivetree and Flowers.

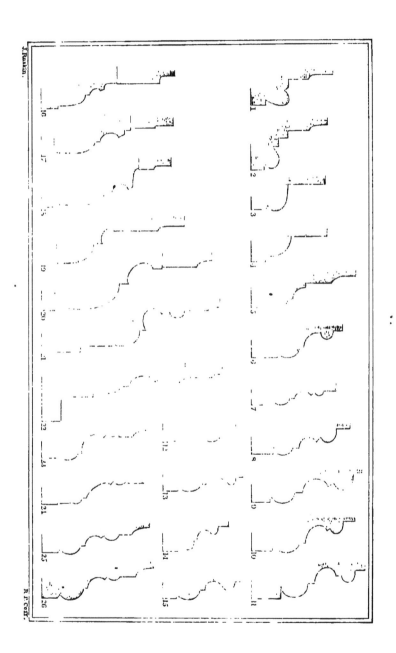

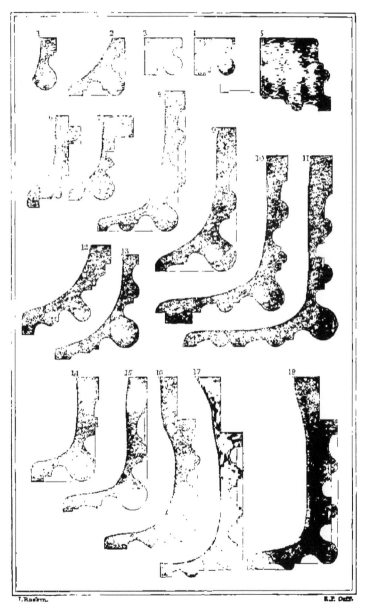

Byzantine Jambs.

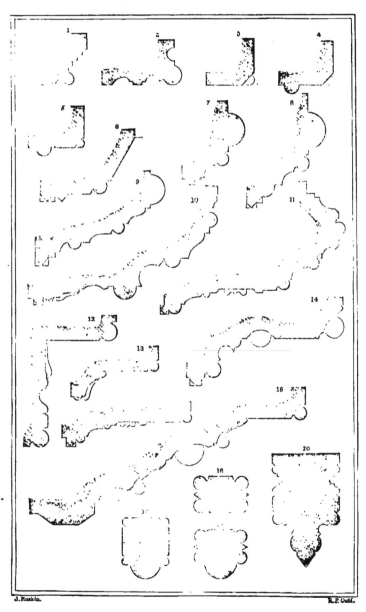

-Gothic Jambs.

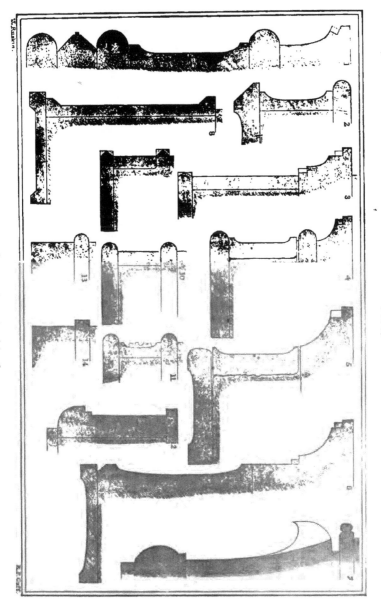

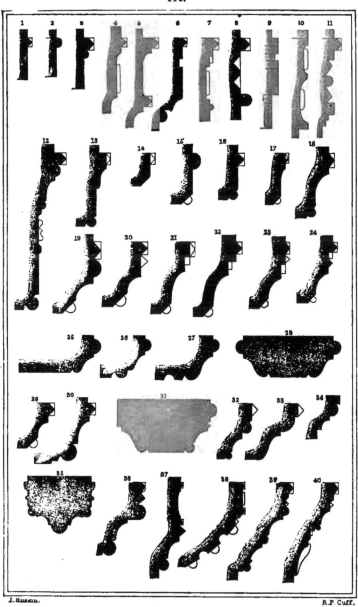

Gothic Archivolts.

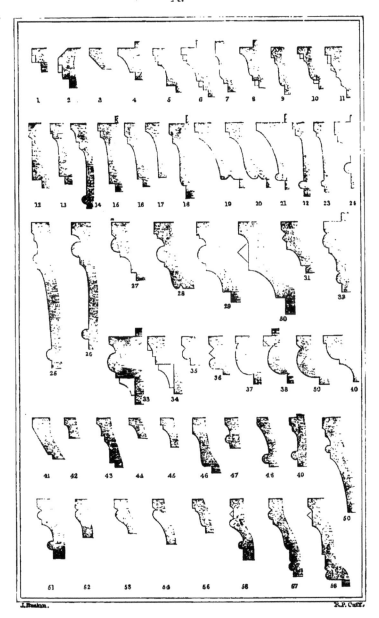

Cornices and Abaci.

Tracery Bars.